The Facts

The Facts

Therese Lloyd

Victoria University Press

VICTORIA UNIVERSITY PRESS
Victoria University of Wellington
PO Box 600 Wellington
vup.victoria.ac.nz

ISBN 9781776561810

Published with the assistance of a grant from

ARTS COUNCIL OF NEW ZEALAND *TOI AOTEAROA*

Printed by Printlink, Wellington

for Lee

Contents

Time

It grows dark as I write now, the clocks have been changed, night comes earlier—gathering like a garment.

—Anne Carson, *Men in the Off Hours*

to begin
with fear
is easy
common and strangely comfortable
hope
however
starts as the voiceless wish
that the pinned down moth
in the specimen drawer
will extract itself
and fly back home
with stories to tell of capture
resistance
and blood-eyed determination
where the slowed down strobes of darkness
entered and exited
where the hot glass ceiling
reflected only her
calm
resolute
gaze

This Time Around

It felt good to have a secret.
Good because it was bad?
Good because it was ours.
We were married before our wedding,
that was the secret.
We tied the knot
at a registry office on Albert Street
Auckland. You held up the flag
and I held you at your waist
pulling you to me.
We see different things in photographs
when we're brave enough to look.
I wore the same dress
at our other wedding
the one with the celebrant
who kept mispronouncing my name,
who told us when we first met her in
a quivery, timid voice
that she was in fact, divorced—
like a chauffeur owning up to a DIC charge.
I was more offended by her sandals.

We faked the signing
at the second wedding
and I faked my signature
on the fake certificate.
I don't know why,
it's hard to fake a signature
and unnecessary, considering.
The night of the second wedding

when everyone had gone
I drove us back
to our friend's bach. We slept, exhausted
on an undressed bed.
I recall a scratchy wool underlay.
A few hours later,
still in my wedding dress,
we drove back to the hall
and started cleaning.

On Metaphysical Insight

Night-time alone suffocates colour. The only way to tackle it
is with thick black oils and reflection. Hopper liked to think his
paintings weren't desolate. 'I'm trying to paint myself,' he said.
The smeared yellow lights of the automat recede to their
     nothingness—
they have to in order to escape the 'illuminated girl of waiting'.
The red line of the shop lino blows itself out in a frowning bowl
     of fruit.
Is it the burning cheeks or the one-gloved hand that keeps us here?
The door keeps opening and closing.

Evenflow

I dreamt about Eddie Vedder
again last night—
this morning, my God, such a spring in my step!
Eddie and I went for a walk down the beach
the tide was out and
although I can't be certain
I think we were in an earthly paradise
he sang to me and I listened and smiled
I was 16 and my 41-year-old knees
did nothing but bend as they should
and the beach didn't end
and the vortex became visible as a solid
and I sidestepped it
and viewed it from every angle
and the stroke forming in my brain
turned into an ampersand
& Eddie and I are still walking

On Looking at Photographs in High School Yearbooks

Young women were much plainer then. Perhaps it was the hair, or the terrible uniforms, or the lack of science in our skin regimes. We wore glasses and had oddly shaped faces and bodies. Uniforms sat on us like the outsized garbage bag squeezed over the top of the Christmas tree I saw once on the side of the road in New York. And then there was Pieta, Jasmine, or Larissa. Each year there was one; a gem-like girl who became my idol. There is a photo of one of them carving a long stick for an art project. I adored her. My plainness bloomed in my teens. Such terrible skin that for years I avoided saying the word 'pore' for fear of drawing attention to myself. I worried about my square face. Knew there was nothing I could do about it. Hated myself for that. There's a photo of me with my best friend. I look happy. I may have been drunk. I'd forgotten that, as a subversive move, I wore ceramic badges on my blazer as a counter attack to the complete lack of any sports or achievement badges. Can lack ever be complete? It seems to me there is always more lack waiting. How?

My mother is not dead. She resides in a room in Christchurch, a city I despise, despite its tragedy. My mother is in a room. Outside her room are other rooms, each one occupied by a single tenant. It would be easy to deduce confinement, banishment, enforced isolation. Will you believe me when I tell you she chose this? That when we packed up her belongings, the most important things to her were the miniature sized tubes of Lancôme products she'd accrued from dozens of gifts with purchase?

In great armfuls I threw away kids' drawings, cards, plaintive letters from overseas. Ribbons and certificates, Tupperware and crockery. Expensive curtains and made-to-measure squabs. The memory of brief wealth lingering in her. Christchurch is winter in my mind always. Cycling to school on frost. A single cigarette bought from the dairy each morning—a 20c Horizon in a lolly bag.

I now own the Kenwood mixer, a three-bar heater, and all her tins of food. My high-school yearbooks brought back to me—a swift eclipse of twenty-eight years.

I was always alone in that room. Imagining no one else could feel the way I did. But the faces of those girls, pulling at their lives, the lack of shimmer, the confusion. All naked and plain. We all had it, even Larissa. Even the beautiful girl with the stick.

Y2K

When I was 'in despair' (the dark days
when I actually used such terms)
I noticed the behaviour of animals—
    sleep when tired, eat when hungry
That made a lot of sense to me
but I felt different
    I felt my humanness too much
No fly ever wonders whether it should make
lots and lots of maggots
    It gives birth on a mound of cat food
or inside the rubbish bin
As far as I know it's not worried
about overpopulation
or what sort of environment its kids
    will grow up in
My humanness sees me at an art gallery
    watching others
        watching walls

My humanness gives me dark thoughts
of cruel behaviour
    You are in the States
a visa glitch and there you remain
    Like Star Trek, I talk to you on a screen
    your face half a second out of sync
with your speech
    I'm in the future
my Tuesday is already over
and I want to tell you all about it
    to prove my superiority

That lovely conceit of time
    that saw people travel from all over the world
to be in Gisborne
    for the first sunrise
        of the new millennium
    Remember
how we all thought the sewer pipes would burst
and the criminals would escape
or something like that
    Y2K packs sent to every household
        because no one knew for certain
        what the number 2000 really meant
Somewhere, people, important people
    waited in bunkers
        fearing the worst

Office at Night

after Edward Hopper

we are all the things
we ignore

the painted lips
dry and fixed

the blind open to a day
that's ended

the forgotten call home
to the other we can't picture

we feed it all day
and it pours out of invisible holes

some part of season is sewn up in this
that time will heal or herald

is for someone else to believe
I'm almost certain I kept it here

a formula, a poem, an address
under the 'miscellany of absence'

and while I look
you look down

a particular strain of shame
that holds us here

Pastoral

The confusing debris of this season
the piles of red pushed up to the curves—
the exploded doneness of the pōhutukawa
How lucky we are to have this gorgeousness!
to witness the slow fade
from scarlet to pink to brown
That nothing disappears
but transmutes
becomes other
is hard for me to remember
I want the brightness of the pōhutukawa blooms
to always burst at the corner of my vision
I don't want to let go
of the angry red
against the overwhelming blue
But one short week
and the path is clogged—
already I'm irritated
by tines in my jandals
and the slackened, spent tree
at my window

The Semiotician in the Dark

They cancelled out the city today
put ropes around it and a blanket over the top
People keep poking around the edges
but not me
I'm reading the signs
That feeling of a day unwinding
its minutes in front of you
the impossibility of this
as though the future had been written
and I'm God's translator
Yet here I am, the world's worker
with sun-smashed skin
and blackened lungs
my job is all our jobs

Desire

The shifty logic of the lover unfolds naturally from his ruses of desire.
—Anne Carson, *Eros the Bittersweet*

Western Motel
after Edward Hopper

That's the grip of someone about to stand
That's the grip of someone about to say
'Right'
The car will take a wide turn
and they will leave the way they came—
her thoughts now, as then
on all the things left undone
Don't put me out here
unseen by everything
except you
Those hills don't protect
they judge
There is no way for me to climb
no access to a thing
that real—you bring me here
to remind
you of
you
you
don't understand outside—
your scenery is conquered dirt
I can't look at what you see
the hard hill grown smooth
through lack of attention—
no one to walk up the sides
to stack stones in a column
at its apex
My house is clean
Take me home

That's the grip of someone who's just arrived
Tentatively, she tests out the bed
for comfort
That straight, alert back
in the room of great angles
light and soft corners
bed-end like a railway sleeper
pillow for a puritan
She is made of blood
she raises herself up
to be seen
There is pioneer in her gaze—
she claims the nakedness
of the hills
as the work of her own hands
She runs those same hands along the wooden bed
remembers the trees
She plants herself here—
My turf, my land

Blindsided

Anne Carson says that eros makes her blind.
Despite the height, she gains no view from the balcony of her writing
  studio—
trapped inside her like some kind of riddle
is the triangle of desire—a distinct shape, constructed forever
of three sides: desire, lack, desiring lack.
It makes less sense each time she thinks of it.
What is eros anyway apart from sore backwards?

The imagined view is polluted but all she wants
really, all she wants
is to roll in its smog
stomp under its acid rain
run and leap over its burning tyres
smoke columns up to the gods.
And I know her,
know when a text is too short
or the air of arbitrary
in her voice down the line—
that something is filling up in her
blocking in the surface of the triangle
that she'd sooner not have.

Wood Tiger Meets Fire Dog

I woke up this morning and my inner animal had metamorphosed.
It's out now. No denying it. I've been awake for three hours and
still no change. 'Each something is a celebration of the nothing that
supports it,' says John Cage. What is to be celebrated here? My meat?
My fur? I expand outward and in a fantastic trick of perspective my
internals shrink, my vitals no longer vital. If I was simply body parts,
you would recognise me easy. But I have complications, post-op
anomalies that bring in curious surgeons from overseas.

The Rottweiler in you, the one that hangs around your neck and
skin-covered thickness, makes me question the advice of parents.
Touching fire is not dangerous. We know what fire does: smokes,
burns, obliterates. Dogs are different. Some are kind. The only way to
find out is to throw a stick for one.

The dog that does not return.
　　The dog that buries the stick.
　　　　The dog that wants you to throw it again and again.

Democratic Moves

My guts are sore and I want to make this list
so that others will remember (on my behalf)
the things that grew from the things that were broken:

On Wednesday I had a matter of urgency to discuss
By Thursday this was no longer urgent
On Friday I had seen the Mona Lisa
By Saturday I regretted the photographs
Six o'clock closing
Monkeys with typewriters
Hamlet's banana errata
A bad chocolate pudding
A movie in the night-morning when sleep was impossible
Cigarettes and no alcohol
Brainwashing marathons
One concrete Buddha
Mum and her scone
Mum and her slice
Mum and her very quiet pills
Expensive makeup to fool everyone who cares
Expensive underwear that God may forgive
A colder winter than the last
And one relentless ocean

Bring me something else
to look at or read. Bring me stories
from the Netherlands, the farthest places
we thought we could never inhabit. Tell me I'm beautiful
because it's clichéd, because it's brave.

This list I thought would be for
you but now that I'm here
I half see the truth—that all this is about
and for and because of me. You
whoever you are, are mostly incidental,
I wish I was sorry for that
but my guts are sore
and there is no time for democracy.

The Soft Body of Desire Creeps Like a Bug Over You

There are layers and levels
that must exist for the burying of matter

The strata of quiet and storm lapping
reads like new information to me

Terrified of all that I don't know
yet it's been lumped inside me

since the moment I was conceived
Where to next? I carried the oversized atlas

back to the Geology Department library—
no one there wanted it. It was outdated and too big to shelve

But the landmasses are still there, the countries still named
How does an atlas become unusable?

The classic quest narrative
set me on a dumb, blind voyage

Desire for the invisible equals trouble every time
Our travel plans to Europe were crooked. You

knew it. I knew it. And the dog too
She shook the bone like it was attached

like it still had blood and flesh. She took the bone
and buried it half-arsed into the earth

Conquering flesh is easy. Close your eyes
now think of Columbus

Imogen

Certain things
I find miraculous
when I remember

That I turned up, bodily
a physical manifestation of me
to that godawful event

I'd promised (faithful to the last)
and despite my beating heart
pulse fading in your hand

I'd gathered.

There is a recording of it, evidence

Signs of miracles
are important to the faithless
stigmata, a vial of moving blood,

saints. My little saint suffered
via her lungs
found it hard to say the word *imagine*

By Sunday

You refused the grapefruit
I carefully prepared
Serrated knife is best
less tearing, less waste
To sever the flesh from the sinew
the chambers where God grew this fruit
the home of the sun, that is
A delicate shimmer of sugar
and perfect grapefruit-sized bowl
and you said, no, God, no
I deflated a little
and was surprised by that
What do we do when we serve?
Offer little things
as stand-ins for ourselves
All of us here
women standing to attention
knives and love in our hands

After Mallarmé

Here we all are, standing on the edge of other people's desires.
—Anne Carson

Poems should echo and reecho against each other . . . They cannot live
alone any more than we can.
—Jack Spicer

French Friends

The sadness in your bones travels like waves
on a river
       It is likely that I caused this
and I'm sorry, but Oh! we were glorious in youth!
        I swanned in and suffocated along with some minor celebrities
Who could have guessed?
       Little lights in the dark
single eyes, and cloud? Yes I blame the war
       for that terrible endless evening
stuck in here, windowless monad
       with all your exquisite blinding mysteries
       I do not know
if evening came first, or escape
       but out there, it's all or nothing
       an invisible soundless fiesta.

Nice Herbs

This is sight-reading for the tone deaf
as of today, I can't decide
whether to live or
y'know, not
It is not without certain quantities of leeway
that the ice around my heart stays solid
The sign has replaced the dinner bell
Very soon the white angels
will eat their greens
despairing inwardly
floating up and over
a space decorated in anger
(they shut out the sunwindow with a TV
and painted the walls a purple bruised kind of plumage)
Nameless ghosts
stop moving through my gizzards!

~~~~~~

~~~~~~~~~~~~~~

~~~~~~~~

~~~~~

stop loitering in my throat!
I'll see you soon enough
the signs are all there.

The Galloper

Funny victory or beautiful suicide?
    You decide
    but
    keep
    me
    out of it
    It's too late
to be tempted by fate but
    I will point you in the right direction
of the now absent tomb
    Somewhere at this minute
some friend presumes treason
    and prescribes fire. It's a delicate thing
your place here
both why and why not
    I'm feeling a bit tragic today
like poor brave Protesilaus
    necessary but forgotten
    and the man upstairs never takes off his shoes
    and their clunk and scrape
dismisses me
    I am the mouse
down here barely
still
someone has to go first.

Open Lady

I was pleased to arrive home to a package
          that I'd worried the man upstairs
would have stolen
          that I'd see him
in a few days
          wearing the hat that I'd ordered
and that I wouldn't have the courage to shout
          'Hey!'
I live in the woulds and this is my problem
          I've been here for a month
and have only just watered the plants
          it's not like me, ask anyone
There is a closed-in part of me
          that thinks laughter sounds like sewing machines
I want to raise my ear to the ceiling
          hear the words those strangers speak
why are they sewing?
          what's so funny?

Printing Crimes

With all the naivety of glue we bulge
  into a new century
just because a coin was tossed
  and death won out
Water is not thirsty, don't forget
  (put that down with your dead friends
  and tributes!)
Too much talk of death
  while the man upstairs plays
Sympathy for the Devil
  on his uke
Take hostages! At least,
  that's what I thought I heard
standing outside some poet's tomb
  feeling the carved letters
of her name blurry under my fingertips.

Spewing (French Friends, second draft)

Oh my dear quartered friend with the face of a flattened hat
      tell me, how do we travel up this spine bone river?

I'm listening, tell me

Some things are too hard—the war, for example, was a real spanner
and what's that line about whistling in the dark?
      I don't need false comfort
      you're here

Yes, some nights are positively Parisian
      and others Paraparaumuian
We fade like centuries, obscure or just ornery as Carson once said
      but that is not someone you know wearing a fake moustache
and swaggering towards you—you don't need to half smile in
      cautious recognition. Just let him mosey on by.

Little Air (Nice Herbs, second draft)

The edge of tomorrow
sounds like a cliché
and yet, what else is daybreak?

All that deciphering in the dark
has made icicles of air
dangerous if you're not careful!

But perhaps these are not signs
souvenirs or symbols
The magnificent dead deliver
letters across the desert
wintercold and bored

Painful blonde at the ice machine
terrible ghosts at the wheel
someone's taken the goose
and her cygnets
but it's too dark to see who.

Yellow Goodbye (The Galloper, second draft)

It's black minims played on a clunky clavier
      (other people are fascinating, don't stare)
There's a thing, an actual phobia of antique furniture
      particularly the Louis XIV stuff, all that scuffed and worn velvet
the dust and bummy smells, the crannies, the etceteras
      I hear it, some kind of movement
a tone or a rhythm echoing across the empty lot
      Is that an angel dressed in 1920s garb
fixing to recite a Spicer poem?
      He's way ahead of his time.
'This one's for the fawn staring at his reflection
      in a bottle of chloroform. I'm pretty, he says
before he falls into a stupor.'

Dirty Sailor (Open Lady, second draft)

Not another dark sad winter?!
   I'm taking myself off to the desert
      just me and the sun
         and all those tiny tiny bits of rock
           Ozymandian delusions gurgle
             in the back of my throat
               like a recently outdated colloquialism
                 It's hella hot out here
                   Dead bouquets gather
                     and echoes of encore
                   peel out thinly in my ear shells

         Just a minute vain friend
                 I see your collection of ancient oils
                  infused with the dreams of bored dogs
            I will not kiss you
          because you blessed me
       when I sneezed
     I am not two inches clear
   of some nameless grave
 but I admit to being tired
and somewhat defunct.

The Tomb of Jack Spicer (Printing Crimes, second draft)

Your friend is dead?
No way! But we sang glory together
our jaws chomping in unison, our throats wide
in victory. Oh well, at least we now have one less
vacant tomb. The minutes are on fire while we wait
for a new dictator. Here comes one now, flaming hat and all.

The Facts

A suddenly arriving beautiful man will not so much fool people as keep
them awake—drunk with our own awakeness we rushed around doing
his bidding.

—Anne Carson

For three months I tried
to make sense of something.
I applied various methods:
logic, illogic, meditation, physical exertion,
starvation, gluttony. Other things too
that are not necessarily the opposite of one another,
writing and reading for example.
But the absurdity of the thing
made all attempt at fact-finding evaporate;
a sort of invisible ink streamed from my pen
the more data I wrote down: facts are things driven,
as Anne Carson says, into a *darkening landscape where other people*
    converse logically.
Even the fact of darkness was one I could not hold on to.
So I tried pushing it into the light. A painting starts with a surface
a place for the visual to gather.
It's a sort of physical square one
where someone I don't know
has obliterated a white surface
with their imagination. We hope to find something there.
Perhaps a bit of ourselves.
I worry too much about what people think
which is why I never draw or paint. Too much me
in that. Too much colour and form.
This surface. I could call it a blueprint

but that has intent and design. This surface is more like air.
I breathe and I live, nothing more or less.
Really, what I am talking about is love. Romantic
love of course needs no elaboration
and yet that is all we ever do. Elaborate
on a thing that breathes now as it did before
and will forever; that is as perennial as the rock
we live on, the calcium in our bones and the iron in our blood.
Chunks of universe circulating in us, yet we get bent up over love.
I have a friend, newly sober, who's taken to astral travel
like you wouldn't believe. He has to find something
to fill in his days, I suppose. Sometimes he tells me where he's been
and I'm always disappointed; like those campground holidays of youth
it's always the same format.
There is a bright light, then movement, then a sense of timelessness
        and void.
He tells me it feels like falling in love. I tell him
I would like to know the feeling of falling out of love.
So far, this has eluded me. I feel the fall
and grip tighter.

*

The surface of a canvas never disappears.
How strange it is to peer through layers of paint
looking for the thing destroyed.
There is an art gallery I visit sometimes.
Nothing ever changes in this gallery. Each painting has a different
        black letter in the bottom right corner.
The letters are not code. Not an anagram
or the initials of the artist. They are marks to remind us
of the failure of language to live up to expectations; that a text message

carries more weight than an epic. Even the colour palette is cynical—
    mustards, and turquoise and shaming lime.
My surface was eclipsed by shadow days of nosleep.
And so a love story begins.

*

Wellness begets wellness. Did you know that?
That a man in a suit who asks for money
on the street will get it. A man in rags will not.
I was well suited up when we met. It was a period
of shimmering I can no more account for
than the fact of déjà vu or telepathy.
Boundlessness streamed from me like the forever movement
of air. I could feel people breathing me in.
When I picture it now, it has a bruised light around it.
Why I narrowed my vision to so small a detail
as you, I don't know. You. Me. The blip of us
is a maddening tick I come back to again and again,
an aberration that fact cannot rectify.
Grey, cold. We had nothing in common. You despised everything
I loved. You voted National. You'd never heard of Anne Carson.
Yet somehow my face was in your hands, your eyes inspecting.
But that is later, first let me tell you how we met.
The first time I saw you I knew you. Actually,
I thought I knew you, and I said to myself, 'Oh. Him.'
Oh him oh him oh him oh him oh him oh him.
For weeks I wracked my brains and still no answer,
and I saw you many times. Each time, something inside me
clicked up a notch. It felt like a kind of novelty gadget
that, I was surprised to find, had its uses.

I preened. In less than a month I had blown my budget
on perfume, clothes, new shoes. I smiled like a thief
at the thought of you.

Carson tells us exactly what desire is, and isn't.
It isn't love letters received and replied to.
It isn't first and second dates. It isn't
meeting family members and weekend trips.
It isn't even passion.
It is a blackened triangle of three equal sides.
It holds its shape in a clutch of fear and longing.
It woos and shames and gnaws. It beats
a retreat at the first sign of failure
only to return the next day for more of the same.
It is a perfect lack of abundance and an abundant lack
of perfection.
When we met,
the triangle
collapsed.

*

To write a poem is to complete a thought.
Jorie Graham says a good poet needs to stay the completion.
Remain, she says, for as long as Houdinily possible.
Trust that your lungs, expansive with air
before you were submerged in the tank, will hold out for as long as the
    poem needs.
To write about us in the past tense forces form
on the formless, parentheses on the eternal. A neat, parabolic air settles
    and makeshift wisdom
takes the place of the real. Yet here I am

dedicating lines to the short glitch of us. I want to complete
this thought. I want this thought to end.

*

You slept on your back,
like a statue, your proportions
were all wrong up close. Winter retreated from you
and came for me instead.
You were the manifestation of something else, something I don't recall
drawing. You were like shadow.
I comforted the cat in the spare room, crowded us both with blankets.
I tried to convince her that everything would be all right,
that this new life is just what we needed. When she ran away
it was a while before I realised what I felt: envy.
Don't ask me why I stayed for as long as I did. Poets
the world over will tell you the same; it takes time to name fear.
Peculiar things seemed to be happening everywhere.
Friends were pairing up with strangers. They were touching
within minutes of meeting. The astral traveller meditated
on his ideal woman and met her that day next to the bucket fountain.
He twirled her around and around in his arms, like a grateful survivor
     from a shipwreck.
What I got was different. It started in my gut first,
a kind of hunger, yet I couldn't eat. No one was worried
because I live on my own, and to live on your own is to hold the secrets
of yourself dear and close.

One short month after it began, it ended.
I heard my phone ring and felt a pellet of cold at the base of my spine.
But the cold did not travel. It stayed there.
For a moment I was intrigued by that small snatch of time it takes

to decide if cold may be hot. But I'm romanticising. The truth is you
    called me
to break my heart so you could hear the sound
of your own power returning. I heard it first.
The roll of swell and bloat. The sickening shriek of victory.
Another woman had won
you as her prize. You had been with her all along, and I was an idiot
for not having suspected.
Love without adoration is a waste of your time. Click. 7.53a.m.
The end. I have not seen your face nor heard your voice since.
But there are facts, and there are facts. In this world I have constructed
I see you every day.
You are the driver and passenger of every car on the motorway.
You are every customer, male and female, in every shop.
You are in every place you do not know of.

Undisputed facts:
You told me many times you loved me (while this was not true as it
    turns out,
it remains a fact).
You were not interested in the night sky.
You told me you were faithful (see above parentheses).
My cat hated you.

*

The something I tried to grasp was cut open then torn up.
From one object
I now had an armful of fragments
with no idea how to arrange them;
on its own, each piece was as meaningless as a single letter.
Huge fat fingers

too cumbersome to push the numbers on a telephone
in an emergency. This is a recurring nightmare of mine,
like the slow-moving pink cement mixer
down the narrow alleyway, and me,
rooted to the spot.
Sleep was the first thing you took.
I would wake every hour until eventually,
four a.m. became my new rising time. The fragments blew about
in a hapless wind. Sleep is refuge and without it, I was exposed. High
on a hill where patterns repeat, I remained, encircled, and still.
Food, the other problem.
Why eat when there's instant coffee and cigarettes?

Whatever the circumstance
(a terrible word but what else was it if not a circumstance?)
a broken heart is always accompanied
by the latent understanding that it is unsustainable.
There is untold evidence of life continuing
despite the fractured state of this vital organ.
Heart. What would love be like if not symbolised by the heart?
If love was liver, or lungs? I love you with all my kidneys.
You have broken my pancreas.
My large intestine belongs to you.

*

Mirror days. Who was speaking to the portrait of me?
She was empty in her skin. Nothing to hold her up but the air of words
she exhaled. She crouched beggar-like in front of a three-bar heater
always in winter with burning knees. She melded. She worried
she was becoming him.

*

Cliché comes from the French word *clicher*. A printmakers' term
    meaning
'to make a stereotype from a relief'.
I know this because Carson told me.
She also told me that you can never leave the mind quickly enough.
Why is it that even with the best teachers in the world,
humans, this human, can still fall down a signposted well?
I became the very breath of cliché.
My rational brain quit.
Rage took over my bowels and bones. It happened
during the terrible storms that I assumed I had caused.
I paced and pored over revenge fantasies,
piling them up like mutton bones,
thinking, I will build a house with these.
Questions formed and toppled like cliff-bound bison.
Which latch in my brain stopped catching?
Was it my Texas-sized ego, deflated and needy that kept me there?
Was it shame?
The corpses formed a deep blood kettle
of counterfactuals and body parts of speech.

*

There grew a slow kind of order.
It started when the cat came back.
Animals understand earthquakes, can feel when the unquiet starts to
    quiet again.
Low slung and guarded, but her sleeping days returned.
She clung to me like a limpet
and made me take cautious steps.

The first of these involved cleaning. I pried open
every secret door, every painted over window. I removed carpets
and clothing, the things that shrouded and supported.
I listened to Beck's *Sea Change* on a crazylady loop.
Stranded in infinity rooms and they're safe from any harm.
When the house was bare, then what?
Vegetables.
I ate food straight from the ground, anything
made of sunlight.

*

When I think of this time, I become very large.
Larger than the life I believe in.
And yet, you know as well as I, thought finds itself in this room in its
*   best moments—*
locked inside its own pressures, fishing up facts of the landscape from
*   notes or memory as well as it may—vibrating (as Mallarmé would*
*   say) with their disappearance.*
It reads to me like a clear perspective on memory's minutiae.
It appears to me like light.
That I zoom in and out with total precision
makes me less scientist and more wizard.
See? I just zapped a cloud right out of the sky.

Absence

The poet is someone who feasts at the same table as other people. But at a certain point he feels a lack. He is provoked by a perception of absence within what others regard as a full and satisfactory present.

—Anne Carson, *Economy of the Unlost*

Mr Anne Carson

I moved all the holiday reading
to the spare room
to keep the literature and the art books
pure
I sat squarely in the middle
of the fluffed-up sunroom sofa, I am
careful
not to disturb the cushions
cushion—a curious word
its function of support
is ancillary to its attractiveness
that's why cushions have covers
in colourful fabric—I become
an ornament
another word I like
because everything here is decoration
everything here is placed
The story of the things here is not new

Sometimes I wish you would come back
Sometimes I miss your absent presence
your book for a face
your pencils for fingers
the way you wore your quest
to become a great man of letters
like a superhero cape
Windows freeze on both sides
you see nothing
when you look out or in
None of this has anything to do with art

or love
I confuse wrong with hard
and still struggle with knowing
what is real
and what is not
I have not been able to find an image
of Anne Carson's first husband anywhere
His beauty almost killed her
I want to see him, maniacally
Everything she wrote about him
may have been a lie
Maybe he didn't steal her poems
maybe he didn't cheat
or have a best friend called Ray
Maybe she, Anne Carson, is him
and her poems
are her confession

Happy Birthday NJ

What about this room? What is in here?
If we stop just before entering
let it be a room
Let there be four walls and a ceiling
The window is for light and to remind
us that we are not alone
that there is always something beyond
Perhaps I am in love with this room
or the love I feel for this room
is greater than what I see out the window
I am anchored here
and I will not describe it to you
All the blood in your veins
could not save you from this room
The light will not save you

What I made in this room
a strange thing
but necessary

Out here, in all this nature
I'm shrinking consciously
So much of me has been absorbed into the atmosphere
Does that make me a legitimate part of the universe now?
Control never really disappears
it's just channelled into something else
I will my will
and it works like a stupid machine

On the weekend
the hippies talked to me about light
and trusting
I smoked and smoked
even in honouring you
I smoked
A eulogy for a living man is not an everyday affair
What apart from the mountains was real there?
The conversations were feathers in the air
and the activities were contrived to seem special
But something happened
in that unreal space
an event like the type we read about
small, non-glorious
but altering

Deep Excavation
Wellington City Gallery, February 2015

Why do I let these people affect me so much?
The living and the dead
this old woman, here, with a cane,
how is it that we can still talk?
All these kids with bung built into their being,
their fears unmasked lying flat
on their faces.
1957 New Zealand, what poor luck.
Today, in a café
listening to overblown music
being served by a kindly waiter,
all this nostalgia is confusing me
too much, never enough. Sometimes
I wish I was not from here.

The Bowmen

On the map you draw a rough square
you go around the square
again and again until
it is deep etched in black
a solid box
You can no longer see where you live
and this is where you live

The small disasters do not add up
to make a catastrophe
The small children do not grow up
to become a family
I hear appliances
applying themselves to their tasks
the sea loud behind them

I sew a button in my mind
I clean out a forgotten drawer
I have grand thoughts of pumpkin soup
What shines at the bottom of the garden
is the myth of having a garden
Out here the giant moon keeps us all quiet
and makes this world I inhabit one big replica

There's not much to gain from living old in a new world
So I leave
I've been told that I'm growing
quietly, like a spruce by a lake
'This morning,' I said
presenting myself to the sky
'I will ignore the lake of sad milk

and the sounds and height
of the outside room
I will provide my own air
and unpack the rings of the broken tree.'
(Out here speech is different
like what a camera sees before it is clicked)

So I take a job acting as salesperson
for the fading light
and no one seems to notice
the group of bowmen lining up on the horizon
They pull and stretch and
shoot their best arrows
and a new 24 hours begins

Image and Influence: Your Me-ness is I-with

The assumption is that if you ask a question, and think about it for long enough, an answer (hopefully the correct one) will arrive. What is an   image is a question-hole that, once in, gets wider and deeper and less   familiar as you go along. Shall we leave the matter there? No, otherwise   nothing would ever come into existence and depending on where you're   standing inside the hole, that's either a good, bad, or blind proposition.   Influence on the other hand, feels like it would be easier to address   somehow (note the words 'feels' and 'somehow'). One way toward an   investigation of influence is through practical experience or experiment.   Let's see. What happens when a poet (you or me, your preference)   decides to spend three years of their grown-up life side by side, arm   in arm with another poet? What happens to your own writing when   this other person (let's call her 'C') takes up a great deal of your thinking   time, both awake and asleep? How does C affect you? First bodily, then   spiritually, then mentally? What happens when you put your pen to   the paper? Is C waiting, ready to stride out onto the page like an   exasperated shopper finally reaching the checkout after a long wait   in the queue? Is there harrumphing? Or does C just tag along, a friend   of a friend who seems nice enough but you forget they're in the car on   the way to the party? Shopping and parties are only one part of it of   course. There are plenty of other things that come into play, not the   least of which is the uncanny fact that your skin really will turn   orange if you eat enough carrots. There's something perfectly childlike   and sensible about that, like if I close my eyes you can no longer see   me. But for three years you did not close your eyes to C. You stared hard right at *her*. You've been in turns hospitable and cold, charitable and disdainful, sycophantic and dismissive. You wish you could say that you and C are close friends but it is true that other people's endlessnesses, their unfathomable fathoms become blinding after a while. A house, now that's a really good analogy. Foundations and floors and walls and ceilings of course, but then there's the pretty work—the facade and front garden, the little fence we spent too long picking a colour for. Everything changes when you live in it, even just for a little while. My mother used to say, 'The more things change, the more they stay the same.' Jean-Baptiste Alphonse Karr wrote that. Neither of us have read him, but that's a line that sticks and picks up debris along the way, and then comes to a very abrupt and fairly uncivil end. A line I'm fond of (and one that my mother has never said) is 'nothing changes if nothing changes'. I wonder what Jean-Baptiste would have to say about that? *Mais bien sûr*! If anyone understands that, of course, it's C. Speaking of parties, I went to one last night. It was interesting. Lots of young people, lots of fedoras. I felt like a curiosity which was mildly pleasant. I drank iced tea and soda water, ate hot chips and smoked a lot of nerve cigarettes. The man you say? Yes, there was a man, someone I don't know who showed next to no interest in me so naturally I was smitten. You see how quickly I forget C? Days like these it's as though she doesn't exist. But I think somehow she would approve. She's all about the dislocation of desire, the violent shove off your axis, the slow regroup and re-establishment of equilibrium. That's her there, over to one side examining the wreckage from another vantage point. This technique means she can create an air of neutrality, like a scientist or an archaeologist, even as she describes prostituting herself to her own husband who has just declared he no longer loves her. She accrues tools along the way to help in her investigations, usually dead writers and painters, their wisdom trapped so they can never create anything new, or, more crucially, defend themselves. Often I hear myself saying things that begin with the phrase 'One day I will . . .' This, I've come to understand, is an effort to show others that I have a clear enough understanding of myself. It's like an assurance that eventually I'll do the right thing. Sometimes it works. Where it fails miserably however is that I become a kind of cancelled equation. I'm neither here nor there, inhabiting a purgatorial space where my movements, forward or back, are contingent on outside factors. Being stuck is peculiar. You know you must move (somehow you know this) and yet you're stuck. It's like trying to jump without bending you knees, impossible. Try it. And this of course is where C returns. Sometimes we need a nudge from an external source in order for physics to take over. And really, who can tell what will happen? I was never encouraged to eat a lot of carrots as a child, but my mother said, if nothing else, my night vision would be excellent. Space and time, energy and force. Really, it's all just a matter of physics. I would never want to reduce C to a conditional binomial random variable or some such thing, but I think she would like the idea of having a physical impact on me. I think she would be able to pick me out from a crowd because of my glowing orange skin. Oh, she'd say, you like carrots too!

Now Here

This morning, seven a.m., the moon was warm
and low—its light on the ocean
was as you'd expect,
and then your image is complete.

I dreamt I was on the top
of an enormous rock,
it was night-time and the moon lit up the scene.
Far below me were my crew
a captain should never abandon her crew
was what I called out to them
before realising I was stuck
with no idea how I got there
nor how to get down.

It's Easter Sunday and autumncold outside
the crispness hasn't happened yet,
it's the undecided season
feet in different quarters,
a time to remember human frailty
that we're all playthings of the weather.
Put me on a mountain
in a thin jacket and rain cloud
and I'm dead within hours,
funny, and we like to think we're not all connected.
You, me, mountain.
Woman's body found, killed by water.

Memoria Verborum

All these surreal images—no
not surreal, just fragmented
It's the nature of memory
to be in bits.
Can memory have a nature?
Can an animal's fear
taint its meat?
I re-collect
I gather
I know
that when I record just one single memory
I make it something else—
your sister running hot tap water over a frozen turkey
Friday night, winter, New Jersey.
Mel, this summer
crowding the night sky with her iPad
using an app that mapped and drew
each constellation.
My sadness at your sadness
had you been there to see it.
But of course you were there,
because those were the days
I took you everywhere
like a large-print A–Z.

Rebound

It shat itself
this morning
the kettle
its electric blue light
pulsing still
but its power somehow enervated
a white, plastic, egg-like nothing—
this is the second kettle to shit itself
in our life together; six years, two kettles.
That obsolescence is built into our appliances
is one of those facts
that we like to get enraged about
then happily go shopping again.
All those shabby appliance repair stores
dotting the suburbs
of the only cities I know,
their hand-painted signs and occasional
flourishes—a grinning cartoon man holds
a smoking TV
a frowning housewife
pushes a broken vacuum cleaner,
the plainness of their names
Thomson Electrical Repairs, and the like—
I can't picture them now.
My mad grandparents
would think me mad
for throwing away a broken kettle
and buying a new one.
That repair is rarely an option
and that the shiny new will always draw me in
because it's easier, because it's there.

Funeral Playlist

There you go, leaving
to be at your father's death bed,
a bit more life shaved off
each day you live.
I haven't met him
and you drive
badly
through the night
past the moon-supporting ocean
armoured up and frightened
of your fears
to be there
when he breathes his last.
In my confusion
and in your neediness
I kissed the black eye
I gave you
and I am not sorry
for your grief
and I will wear my best dress
Please note, I'd like
'Into My Arms',
'Here's Where the Story Ends'
and 'Avalon' too, if there's time.

A Day, January

Yesterday.
That's when it was, so let's look at that.
In the muted sun on the sharp-shelled beach
all the broken pieces
yet nothing pierced the skin of my feet
the sharpness cancelled out
to a homogeneous rubble.
I walked home from the karakia
I walked a long way, the furthest I've been able to
since my spine decided to twist itself in the wrong direction.
Backs take the strain of the invisible things
the harder they are to see, the heavier they are to carry.

I walked towards the dot of my house
carrying that image
of eleven young men
trying to lift a tree trunk
out of the wet sand
of a beach that couldn't care less.
That severed trunk wasn't defiant, or obtuse.
It had no intention to kill when it stranded itself
unclenched from the ground by a storm. And the thing
that made it impossible for those men to move it,
the water, lapping, pulsing up around them as they heaved breathless
had already begun, a slow disposal, a gradual return.

King of the Wood

after Graham Fletcher

You have come with me
from island to island, house to house
cut in three places, your new head still new
in a treeless landscape of indifferent grass
The Big Mute
I would lie you down
if it weren't for your roots
invisible and no doubt troubled and long
But you hold your space
and make a shadow there

There's a smear on your surface
where a friend leaned her greasy head
do you mind like I do?
Proud sad phallus with no hands to touch
and that live-dead tear
making its way to nowhere
on your zeppelin face
Why so sad Woody? You've got one eye
to see the sea
and to watch me looking at you
I want to exit this place
come over the dead horizon of your home
and live with you there

'Light and things'

after Bill Culbert

The dark, secret relations of opposites
the mutual distrust, the absolute dependency.
For example,
I can only walk backwards
if I understand which way is forwards.

In this room filled with light
I don't trust myself.
I stay low—adhere to the detritus, the wrong
effects of us in the world.

I move
slowly
like I'm climbing a horizontal ladder.
For comfort, I read
words on plastic bottles
foreign words
that exoticise the ordinary
eau de javel, mon chéri.

When you left, you took all manner of things,
light was the least of my worries.

Why did I bring you with me today?
I watch you through Venetian blinds
clandestine, suspect
and then its opposite,
brazen, like I'm in an 80s music video.

I keep finding fragments
of us,
always something there to remind me
da da da dah dah
so I've catalogued them all around the edges of the sunroom
memento mori—things to step over
because light travels whether your eyes are opened or closed
because today I feel transfixed—
it happens sometimes—out of nowhere
I don't expect
you to understand. When you left you took
all the sharp implements, so this vague talk of impalement
will be surprising to you.

When I save these words I'm reminded
this product is licenced to you.

I count. I count suspended chairs and tables.
In their quiet chaos, a hard angle.
I came to believe
in a God
that threw them in a rage—
some celestial tantie to teach us humans a lesson
perhaps that my comfort should not be assumed.

The attendant circles
as though writing steals something,
and she's right to be suspicious.
Perhaps I'm stealing this stillness,
perhaps I'm trying to make
an invisible support
for the Atlas we forget is there.

That you still
rise to the surface, bob
and rock, almost comical in your unannounced entrances
shakes me,
and anchors me to whatever spot
I'm in.

Roast Lamb for Christmas Dinner, For Example

when I think of temporary things
like this broken pencil
that breaks more with each word
or the marriage that I had once
and then didn't, or
the way my father
drank gin and tonic for breakfast
on the last days of his life
and the thing under the car
that's missing, dropped off no doubt
on some road I travel daily
and I don't know
I just don't know
if it's the lack of you
or you, or the sidelong wink
to the three bottles of chardonnay
lined up like sunny wise men
oh husband—Jesus Christ?
you are the lamb
in the bible, the hilarious
jewel-encrusted lamb
spiralling around in the spiritual ecstasies
of our Lord
and we all know how that ended
how strange we all are
mixing up our stories
and getting things right and wrong
roast lamb for Christmas dinner, for example.

Eleven a.m.

after Edward Hopper

I am only as big as the light
     from my skin.
          I send it out searching
              for other open windows
and I'm ready
to go.

I am the Duchess of Dirty Laundry and Hapless Mortals
     my realm is made up of minutes
          taken and given
              where activities fold over themselves
in incremental shifts
of light from my skin

When I took my throne
     time began
          I am waiting to see
              what will happen
when I stand.

Notes on the poems

The poems in this book were written as part of my doctoral thesis, which examined the ekphrastic poetry of Canadian poet and classicist Anne Carson. As such, I owe a great debt to Carson. Quotations from several of her books and a liberal borrowing of some of her rhetorical strategies are threaded throughout *The Facts*.

In homage to Carson, I have deliberately misquoted her (she's a trickster like that) in the epigraph to the poem sequence 'After Mallarmé'. The original sentence comes from *Eros the Bittersweet* (1986) and reads, 'Something paradoxical is inherent in these shifts, and as readers, we are invited into its experience, standing on the edge of other people's desire, arrested, wooed, triangulated and changed by a series of marks on a piece of paper.'

Acknowledgements

Thank you to all of the lovely people who graciously gave me their time, support and friendship during the writing of these poems. Thanks to Pip, Roisin, Emma, Neil, Mike, Peter, Lucy, Bianca, Kelly, Eve, Renee, Jeremy, Malcolm, Diane and so many more. A special thank you to my dear friend Hilda Daw whose friendship has been nothing short of transformative. Thank you to my PhD cohort and all the fine folk at the IIML and to my supervisors Harry Ricketts and Marco Sonzogni. Thank you also to Greg Lloyd, Celia Jenkins, Jack Ross, Wendy Key, Jane Blackmore, Paula Collier, Eli Foley, Simeon Collier-Foley, Tracey Hall, Andy Hummel, Kiki van Newtown, Vanessa Stacey, Kalya Ward. Thanks to my sister Bronwyn for her perennial support, whether it be offering critical feedback and advice, painting out an aubergine feature wall, or dropping everything to be with me at the funeral of my beloved Sylvie.

Thank you especially to Martin Farmer for arriving when you did.

Most of all, thank you to Lee Posna. We've navigated the hardest transition of all—from husband and wife to dear friends. Thank you for your friendship, your poetry, and for being here. Semper amici.

In memory of Sylvie, 2009–2017